33 DAY CONSECRATION TO JESUS THROUGH MARY

Compiled by
John Pridmore & Niall Slattery

D1603354

*All booklets are published
thanks to the generosity of the supporters
of the Catholic Truth Society*

Contents

All rights reserved. First published 2015 by The Incorporated Catholic Truth Society, 42-46 Harleyford Road London SE11 5AY Tel: 020 7640 0042 Fax: 020 7640 0046. © 2015 The Incorporated Catholic Truth Society.

ISBN 978 1 78469 032 8

Introduction

St Louis de Montfort in his thirty-three-day consecration (*Total Consecration to Jesus through Mary*) helps us to consecrate our hearts and all that we have to the Immaculate Heart of Mary, and through her heart to the Most Sacred Heart of Jesus.

This devotion has helped me to understand the depth of the love of Mary and Jesus in a way that I didn't think was possible. There is a supernatural grace in this consecration that I feel is beyond human words or understanding. The late Holy Father St John Paul II stated that through reading this consecration his life was transformed. He said, "this Marian devotion has since remained an integral part of my interior life and of my spiritual theology".

I believe that this devotion is truly life-changing and brings us to a deep foundation built on the rock of Christ. It protects us in this world of spiritual warfare and helps us to understand the gifts given us by God the creator.

I would advise that before starting this devotion you pray for the grace of perseverance and give it your fullest attention and time, because in spiritual warfare the enemy will try everything to rob you of these incredible graces. The protection prayer on page 6 is a good prayer for each day of this devotion.

Each day consists of an opening prayer, a scripture reading, a reading from the writings of St Louis de Montfort, a reflection and various prayers. It is recommended that you finish this devotion on a Marian feast day, so before you start, check the calendar of possible consecration dates for the best day to begin.

St Louis de Montfort speaks of a remnant Marian army that will bring immeasurable graces to heaven, and I believe, as St Louis de Montfort did, that this consecration is the commissioning to that army. I cannot recommend it highly enough.

John Pridmore

St Louis de Montfort

St Louis Grignon de Montfort (1673-1716) was a French diocesan priest with a great devotion to the Virgin Mary. He was born in Brittany, and ordained priest in Paris in 1700. He spent his life working with the poor and the sick, and as an itinerant missionary in Poitiers and Brittany. He was famous for his fervent and enthusiastic preaching and apostolate. He founded an order of missionary priests, the Company of Mary, and a sister order of nuns, the Daughters of Wisdom. He is best known, however, for his book *True Devotion to the Blessed Virgin Mary*, which like most of his writings was not properly published until the nineteenth century. It proposes that the Christian make a "total consecration" of himself to Jesus through Mary; it has had an immense influence, not least on St John Paul II.

St Louis was canonised in 1947. His feast day is 28th April.

Healing and Protection Prayer

Heavenly Father, I praise and thank You for all You have given me. Please cover me with the protective, precious blood of Your Son Jesus Christ. Increase Your Holy Spirit in me with His gifts of wisdom, knowledge, understanding, hunger for prayer, guidance and discernment to help me know Your will and surrender to it more completely.

Father, please heal my negative emotions and any wounds in my heart and spirit. Send the sword of Your Holy Spirit to sever and break all spells, curses, hexes, voodoo and all negative genetic, intergenerational and addictive material, past, present or to come, known or unknown, against me, my relationships and family, finances, possessions and ministry.

Father, I forgive and I ask forgiveness for my sins and failings, and I ask that my whole person, body and mind, heart and will, soul and spirit, memory and emotions, attitudes and values lie cleansed, renewed and protected by the most precious blood of Your Son, Jesus.

In the name, power, blood and authority of Jesus Christ I bind and break the power and effect in or around me of any and all evil spirits who are trying to harm me in any way, and I command these spirits and their companion spirits in the name of the Father, the Son, and the Holy Spirit to leave me peacefully and quietly and go immediately and directly to the Eucharistic presence of Jesus Christ in the closest Catholic Church tabernacle to be disposed of by Jesus and never again return to harm me.

Dear Holy Spirit, please fill up any void in me to overflowing with your great love. All this, Father, I pray in the name of Jesus Christ by the guidance of Your Holy Spirit. Immaculate heart of Mary spouse of the Holy Spirit, please pray for and with me.

Amen.

DAYS 1-12: Renouncing the Spirit of the World for the Spirit of the Gospel

St Louis de Montfort writes, "Those who desire to take up this devotion should spend at least twelve days emptying themselves of the spirit of the world, which is opposed to the Spirit of Jesus".

These coming days we will undertake to rid ourselves of the spirit of the world by prayer, fasting and almsgiving. For the rest of our lives we will battle against this spirit that prevails in our modern culture and society to put on the Spirit of Christ in which we were baptised.

St Louis de Montfort teaches that through self-denial we can find power to overcome and renounce the spirit of the world. By putting ourselves last, we are enabled to put God and others first, and, by doing so, help root out our preoccupation with self, materialistic values, pride and vanities. These twelve days help mould us into having a love of God's commandments and obedience to his will. It brings us out of darkness of mind and spirit, seduction and corruption, to the light, freedom and clarity of the Holy Spirit.

Day 1: Renouncing the Spirit of the World

Theme: **Trusting in God and his Providence**

Opening Prayer

Come Holy Spirit, come by means of the powerful intercession of the Immaculate Heart of Mary your well-beloved spouse. (*3 times*)

Scripture

Jesus said, 'That is why I am telling you not to worry about your life and what you are to eat, nor about your body and how you are to clothe it. Surely life means more than food, and the body more than clothing! Look at the birds in the sky. They do not sow or reap or gather into barns; yet your heavenly Father feeds them.' (*Mt* 6:25-26)

Reading from St Louis de Montfort

The grace of God is absolutely necessary

Chosen soul, living image of God and redeemed by the precious blood of Jesus Christ, God wants you to become holy like him in this life, and glorious like him in the next. It is certain that growth in the holiness of God is your vocation. All your thoughts, words, actions, everything you suffer or undertake must lead you towards that end.

Dust into light, uncleanness into purity, sinfulness into holiness, creature into Creator, man into God! A marvellous work, I repeat, so difficult in itself, and even impossible for a mere creature to bring about, for only God can accomplish it by giving his grace abundantly and in an extraordinary manner. The very creation of the universe is not as great an achievement as this.[1]

Reflection

A man once said, "In my own life I have found that in trusting God and opening my heart to his providence, he is a God who is never outdone with his generosity. The more I have learned to give and not hold anything back, the more it seems to give God permission to pour out an abundance of grace and blessings in my everyday life. We cannot be too generous."

"It is not enough to give, we are called to give until it hurts." (Blessed Mother Teresa)

Resolution

As we begin this period of preparation it is necessary for us to decide how much time we will put aside each day for personal prayer and reflection. This must be a commitment we intend to keep for the entire thirty-three days.

Let us ask the Blessed Virgin Mary for the grace to be generous as God is generous.

Recite the prayers for the day listed on page 92.

Day 2: Renouncing the Spirit of the World

Theme: **God is the foundation of our lives**

Opening Prayer

Come Holy Spirit, come by means of the powerful intercession of the Immaculate Heart of Mary your well-beloved spouse. (*3 times*)

Scripture

Jesus said, 'Therefore, everyone who listens to these words of mine and acts on them will be like a sensible man who built his house on rock.' (*Mt* 7:24)

Reading from St Louis de Montfort

Chosen soul, how will you bring this about? What steps will you take to reach the high level to which God is calling you? The means of holiness and salvation are known to everybody, since they are found in the gospel; the masters of the spiritual life have explained them; the saints have practised them and shown how essential they are for those who wish to be saved and attain perfection. These means are: sincere humility, unceasing prayer, complete self-denial, abandonment to divine Providence, and obedience to the will of God.[2]

Reflection

Personal prayer is where we bore into the rock of Jesus and plant our roots firmly in God's foundation. There can be no substitute. The more we pray, the more we give God permission to bless our lives.

"Give God permission." (Blessed Mother Teresa)

Resolution

Ask Our Lady for a deep desire to rid ourselves of all attachments that hold us back from a closer relationship with God, and to commit to more personal prayer time.

Recite the prayers for the day listed on page 92.

Day 3: Renouncing the Spirit of the World

Theme: Jesus Christ was born into poverty for my sake, so that I might be redeemed from my brokenness and sins.

Opening Prayer

Come Holy Spirit, come by means of the powerful intercession of the Immaculate Heart of Mary your well-beloved spouse. (*3 times*)

Scripture

Peter said, 'We have left everything and followed you.' Jesus said, 'I tell you solemnly, there is no one who has left house, brothers, sisters, mother, father, children or land for my sake and for the sake of the gospel who will not be repaid a hundred times over, houses, brothers, sisters, mothers, children and land - not without persecutions - now in this present time and, in the world to come, eternal life.' (*Mk* 10:28-30)

Reading from St Louis de Montfort

The necessity of mortification

The Holy Spirit tells us that Wisdom is not found in the hearts of those who live in comfort (*Jb* 28:13), gratifying their passions and bodily desires, because "they who are of the flesh cannot please God", and "the wisdom of the flesh is an enemy to God" (*Rm* 8:8,7). All those who belong to Christ, incarnate Wisdom, have crucified their flesh with its passions and desires. They always bear about in their bodies the dying of Jesus. They continually carry their cross daily. They are dead and indeed buried with Christ (*Ga* 5:24; *2 Co* 4:10; *Lk* 9:23; *Rm* 6:4,8). These words of the Holy Spirit show us more clearly than the light of day that, if we are to possess incarnate Wisdom, Jesus Christ, we must practise self-denial and renounce the world and self.[3]

Reflection

When we sacrifice we open a door to the possibility of God's grace, and the more we sacrifice the bigger that door becomes. The lives of the saints show that the more we give to God, the more miracles he is able to perform.

> "The two mortifications that God can never refuse are fasting from food and fasting from sleep." (St John Vianney)

Resolution

Ask Our Blessed Mother for the grace to renounce some comfort and make sacrifices for the sake of the Kingdom of God.

Recite the prayers for the day listed on page 92.

Day 4: Renouncing the Spirit of the World

Theme: **Making time for God**

Opening Prayer

Come Holy Spirit, come by means of the powerful intercession of the Immaculate Heart of Mary your well-beloved spouse. (*3 times*)

Scripture

Jesus said, 'When you pray, do not imitate the hypocrites: they love to say their prayers standing up in the synagogues and at the street corners for people to see them. I tell you solemnly, they have had their reward. But when you pray, go to your private room and, when you have shut your door, pray to your Father who is in that secret place, and your Father who sees all that is done in secret will reward you.' (*Mt* 6:5-6)

Reading from St Louis de Montfort

Wondrous to relate, this divine Wisdom chose to leave the bosom of his Father and enter the womb of a virgin and there repose amid the lilies of her purity. Desiring to give himself to her by becoming man in her, he sent the archangel Gabriel to greet her on his behalf and to declare to her that she had won his heart and he would become man within her if she gave her consent. The archangel fulfilled his mission and assured her that she would still remain a virgin while becoming a mother. Notwithstanding her desire to be lowly, Mary wholeheartedly gave the angel that priceless consent which the Blessed Trinity, all the angels and the whole world awaited for so many centuries. Humbling herself before her Creator she said, "Behold the handmaid of the Lord. Let it be done to me according to your word."[4]

Reflection

Do you want to know what God wants? He wants your everything! He wants us to give him permission to run our lives in every area. When we find the pearl of great price, which is the love of God for us, we should be willing to exchange everything for that pearl. On many occasions people try to be in control because they are under the illusion that this will keep them safe and secure, but in truth they become prisoners because they do not allow God to be in control and do not trust him. When we learn to let go, we start to experience the freedom God created us for.

"I want you to be happy, always happy in the Lord; I repeat, what I want is your happiness." (*Ph* 4:4)

Resolution

Ask Our Lady for the grace to surrender to God's will in all things.

Recite the prayers for the day listed on page 92.

Day 5: Renouncing the Spirit of the World

Theme: Our prayers should not be self-seeking, but should lead us to say "thy will be done"

Opening Prayer

Come Holy Spirit, come by means of the powerful intercession of the Immaculate Heart of Mary your well-beloved spouse. (*3 times*)

Scripture

Jesus said, 'So you should pray like this: Our Father in heaven, may your name be held holy, your kingdom come, your will be done, on earth as in heaven. Give us today our daily bread. And forgive us our debts, as we have forgiven those who are in debt to us. And do not put us to the test, but save us from the evil one.' (*Mt* 6:9-13)

Reading from St Louis de Montfort

Nothing is more consoling than to know divine Wisdom. Happy are those who listen to him; happier still are those who desire him and seek him; but happiest of all are those who keep his laws. Their hearts will be filled with that infinite consolation which is the joy and happiness of the eternal Father and the glory of the angels (cf. *Pr* 2:1-9). If only we knew the joy of a soul that perceives the beauty of divine Wisdom and is nourished with the milk of divine kindness, we would cry out with the bride in the Song of Songs: "Your love is better than wine" (*Sg* 1:3) better by far than all created delights. This is especially true when divine Wisdom says to those who contemplate him, "Taste and see" (*Ps* 33:9), eat and drink, be filled with my eternal sweetness (*Sg* 5:1), for you will discover that conversing with me is in no way distasteful, that my companionship is never tedious and in me only will you find joy and contentment (*Ws* 8:16).[5]

Reflection

People often pray for their family and those closest to them but do not ask God what he wants them to pray for. When we really reflect on what God wants us to pray for we move into a realm of deep contemplation and a world changing openness to the guidance of God and his Holy Spirit.

"Prayer and fasting can avert wars."
(Our Lady of Fatima)

Resolution

Ask Our Blessed Mother to help us pray as God would want.

Recite the prayers for the day listed on page 92.

Day 6: Renouncing the Spirit of the World

Theme: Jesus took the path of self-sacrifice to show us the way

Opening Prayer

Come Holy Spirit, come by means of the powerful intercession of the Immaculate Heart of Mary your well-beloved spouse. (*3 times*)

Scripture

Then to all he said, 'If anyone wants to be a follower of mine, let him renounce himself and take up his cross every day and follow me. For anyone who wants to save his life will lose it; but anyone who loses his life for my sake, that man will save it. What gain, then, is it for a man to have won the whole world and to have lost or ruined his very self?' (*Lk* 9:22-25)

Reading from St Louis de Montfort

My dear brothers and sisters, there are two companies that appear before you each day: the followers of Christ and the followers of the world. Our dear Saviour's company is on the right, climbing up a narrow road, made all the narrower by the world's immorality. Our Master leads the way, barefooted, crowned with thorns, covered with blood, and laden with a heavy cross. Those who follow him, though most valiant, are only a handful, either because his quiet voice is not heard amid the tumult of the world, or because people lack the courage to follow him in his poverty, sufferings, humiliations and other crosses which his servants must carry all the days of their life. Do you listen to the voice of Jesus who, burdened with his Cross, calls out to you, "Come after me; anyone who follows me will not be walking in the dark; be brave; I have conquered the world."[6]

Reflection

A man once had a dream, where he was trying to drive a car. Every time he tried to turn the wheel he could not control it. Then he heard the words "Let go!", and the car took him to the most wonderful places he could ever imagine. He realised if he allowed God to direct his life and give up his agenda, God would take him on a "Fantastic Adventure In Trusting Him": "F.A.I.T.H.".

> "When you were young you put on your own belt and walked where you liked; but when you grow old you will stretch out your hands, and somebody else will put a belt round you and take you where you would rather not go." (*Jn* 21:18)

Resolution

Ask our Blessed Mother for the grace to not be afraid of the cross but to embrace it as her Son did.

Recite the prayers for the day listed on page 92.

Day 7: Renouncing the Spirit of the World

Theme: Repentance and Conversion

Opening Prayer

Come Holy Spirit, come by means of the powerful intercession of the Immaculate Heart of Mary your well-beloved spouse. (*3 times*)

Scripture

Jesus said, 'What man among you with a hundred sheep, losing one, would not leave the ninety-nine in the wilderness and go after the missing one till he found it? And when he found it, would he not joyfully take it on his shoulders and then, when he got home, call together his friends and neighbours? "Rejoice with me," he would say "I have found my sheep that was lost." In the same way, I tell you, there will be more rejoicing in heaven over one repentant sinner than over ninety-nine virtuous men who have no need of repentance.' (*Lk* 15:4-7)

Reading from St Louis de Montfort

The Gospel teaches us that a sinner who is converted and who does penance gives joy to all the angels. If the repentance and conversion of one sinner is enough to make the angels rejoice, how great must be the happiness and jubilation of the whole heavenly court and what glory for our Blessed Lord himself to see us here on earth meditating devoutly and lovingly on his humiliations and torments and on his cruel and shameful death! Let us meditate, then, on the life and sufferings of our Saviour by means of the holy Rosary; let us learn to know him well and to be grateful for all his blessings, so that, on the Day of Judgement, he may number us among his children and his friends.[7]

Reflection

Each time we taste the mercy of Christ in the sacrament of confession we are renewed and made whole, healed and given all the graces we need to continue on our journey. We also meet Christ personally: "Go in peace; your sins are forgiven."

> "Sooner would heaven and earth fade away than anyone asking for my mercy be turned away." (Jesus to St Faustina)

Resolution

Make time for an examination of conscience and make a commitment to attend the Sacrament of Confession with an open and sincere heart.

Recite the prayers for the day listed on page 92.

DAY 8: Renouncing the Spirit of the World

Theme: Depend upon Christ and do not be tied down by worldly success or esteem

Opening Prayer

Come Holy Spirit, come by means of the powerful intercession of the Immaculate Heart of Mary your well-beloved spouse. (*3 times*)

Scripture

And there was a man who came to him and asked, 'Master, what good deed must I do to possess eternal life?' Jesus said to him, 'Why do you ask me about what is good? There is one alone who is good. But if you wish to enter into life, keep the commandments.' He said, 'Which?' 'These:' Jesus replied, 'You must not kill. You must not commit adultery. You must not bring false witness. Honour your father and mother; and you must love your neighbour as yourself.' The young man said to him, 'I have kept all these. What more do I need to do?' Jesus said, 'If you wish to be perfect, go and sell what you own and give the money to the poor, and you will have treasure in heaven; then come, follow me.' But when the young man heard these words he went away sad, for he was a man of great wealth. (*Mt* 19:16-22)

Reading from St Louis de Montfort

If we can conceive on earth no employment more lofty than the service of God - if the least servant of God is richer, more powerful and more noble than all the kings and emperors of this earth, unless they also are the servants of God - what must be the riches, the power and the dignity of the faithful and perfect servant of God, who is devoted to his service entirely and without reserve, to the utmost extent possible?

Such is the faithful and loving slave of Jesus in Mary who has given himself up entirely to the service of that King of Kings, by the hands of his holy Mother, and has reserved nothing for himself. Not all the gold of earth nor all the beauties of the heavens can repay him.[8]

Reflection

St Francis of Assisi is a saint who knew what it was not to be weighed down by worldly possessions. Often in life we think materialistic wealth gives us security, but it is God alone who is our security. It is fine to own good things, but it is not fine for good things to own us.

"If you are born in poverty, embrace your poverty. If you are born in immense wealth embrace that position. But always surrender to the will of God and be generous." (Blessed Mother Teresa)

Resolution

Ask Our Lady for the grace to be generous in our response to God's call.

Recite the prayers for the day listed on page 92.

Day 9: Renouncing the Spirit of the World

Theme: **Seeking to live a godly life**

Opening Prayer

Come Holy Spirit, come by means of the powerful intercession of the Immaculate Heart of Mary your well-beloved spouse. (*3 times*)

Scripture

Then he began to speak. This is what he taught them: 'How happy are the poor in spirit: theirs is the kingdom of heaven. Happy the gentle: they shall have the earth for their heritage. Happy those who mourn: they shall be comforted. Happy those who hunger and thirst for what is right: they shall be satisfied. Happy the merciful: they shall have mercy shown them. Happy the pure in heart: they shall see God.' (*Mt* 5:2-8)

Reading from St Louis de Montfort

It is difficult to persevere in holiness because of the excessively corrupting influence of the world. The world is so corrupt that it seems almost inevitable that religious hearts be soiled, if not by its mud, at least by its dust. It is something of a miracle for anyone to stand firm in the midst of this raging torrent and not be swept away, to weather this stormy sea and not be drowned, or robbed by pirates; to breathe this pestilential air and not be contaminated by it. It is Mary, the singularly faithful Virgin over whom Satan had never any power, who works this miracle for those who truly love her.[9]

Reflection

We live in a world where sexual immorality is paraded and pushed on us, as if to live without it would not be possible. When we desire a pure heart for God we put on a helmet of morality which cleanses our mind, purifies our heart and brings great joy to Jesus.

"God does not ask for success, only faithfulness." (Blessed Mother Teresa)

Resolution

Let us implore Our Lady's help to try and seek God's kingdom with all our hearts.

Recite the prayers for the day listed on page 92.

Day 10: Renouncing the Spirit of the World

Theme: **We serve God first**

Opening Prayer

Come Holy Spirit, come by means of the powerful intercession of the Immaculate Heart of Mary your well-beloved spouse. (*3 times*)

Scripture

But when the Pharisees heard that he had silenced the Sadducees, they got together and, to disconcert him, one of them put a question. 'Master, which is the greatest commandment of the Law?' Jesus said, 'You must love the Lord your God with all your heart, with all your soul, and with all your mind. This is the greatest and the first commandment. The second resembles it: You must love your neighbour as yourself. On these two commandments hang the whole Law, and the Prophets also.' (*Mt* 22:34-40)

Reading from St Louis de Montfort

Oh! How happy is the man who has given everything to Mary, and has trusted himself to Mary in everything and for everything! He belongs all to Mary, and Mary belongs all to him. He can say boldly with David, "Mary is made for me;" or with the beloved disciple, "I have taken her for my own" or with Jesus Christ, "All that I have is yours, and all that you have is mine."[10]

Reflection

When we choose to follow God there are many people who seem to try and take us away from God's plan. It is very easy to listen to these people and adopt their point of view. We have to realise we do not follow people, we follow only God, and often if we seek the advice of people who are caught up in the world and its brokenness, the wisdom we will receive is a worldly wisdom, which is not wisdom at all, but foolishness. Often if we speak to people about what God's plan for them is, they quote what their friends or parents think. This can be a great blockage to us seeking and desiring what God wants. If we are to ask advice of people, let us first make sure that they are people of God. But most of all let us make sure that we ask God first.

"I die the king's good servant, but God's first." (St Thomas More)

Resolution

Let us ask Mary for the grace to say yes to God in all that he asks, just as she herself did.

Recite the prayers for the day listed on page 92.

Day 11: Renouncing the Spirit of the World

Theme: **Seeking what is important to God**

Opening Prayer

Come Holy Spirit, come by means of the powerful intercession of the Immaculate Heart of Mary your well-beloved spouse. (*3 times*)

Scripture

Pure, unspoilt religion, in the eyes of God our Father, is this: coming to the help of orphans and widows when they need it, and keeping oneself uncontaminated by the world. (*Jm* 1:27)

Reading from St Louis de Montfort

Being the way by which Jesus Christ came to us the first time, Mary will also be the way by which he will come the second time, though not in the same manner. Being the sure means and the straight and immaculate way to go to Jesus Christ, and to find him perfectly, it is by her that the holy souls, who are to shine forth especially in sanctity, have to find Our Lord. He who shall find Mary shall find life; that is, Jesus Christ, who is the Way, the Truth, and the Life. But no one can find Mary who does not seek her; and no one can seek her, who does not know her: for we cannot seek or desire an unknown object. It is necessary, then, for the greater knowledge and glory of the Most Holy Trinity, that Mary should be more known than ever. Mary must shine forth more than ever in mercy, in might, and in grace, in these latter times: in mercy, to bring back and lovingly receive the poor strayed sinners who shall be converted and shall return to the Catholic Church.[11]

Reflection

The witness of Mother Teresa is a witness of someone who learned what it is to give until it hurts. Many people in life look to be healed and free. The way we receive these gifts is by giving. The more we give the more we receive and the greatest gift that Jesus can give us is the gift of love for your neighbour and love for yourself.

Lord, make me an instrument of your peace. Where there is hatred, let me sow love; where there is injury, pardon; where there is doubt, faith; where there is despair, hope; where there is darkness, light; where there is sadness, joy.

O Divine Master, grant that I may not so much seek to be consoled as to console; to be understood as to understand; to be loved as to love; for it is in giving that we receive; it is in pardoning that we are pardoned; it is in dying that we are born again to eternal life. (Peace prayer of St Francis)

Resolution

Ask Our Lady to help us see the needs of others before our own.

Recite the prayers for the day listed on page 92.

Day 12: Renouncing the Spirit of the World

Theme: **We are called and chosen, to be set apart from the world**

Opening Prayer

Come Holy Spirit, come by means of the powerful intercession of the Immaculate Heart of Mary your well-beloved spouse. (*3 times*)

Scripture

Jesus said, 'I have made your name known to the men you took from the world to give me. They were yours and you gave them to me, and they have kept your word. Now at last they know that all you have given me comes indeed from you; for I have given them the teaching you gave to me, and they have truly accepted this, that I came from you, and have believed that it was you who sent me. I pray for them; I am not praying for the world but for those you have given me, because they belong to you.' (*Jn* 17:6-9)

Reading from St Louis de Montfort

Eternal Wisdom, besides being the object of the eternal Father's delight, and the joy of angels, is also the source of purest joy and consolation for man who possesses him. He gives to man a relish for everything that comes from God and makes him lose his taste for things created. He enlightens his mind with the brightness of his own light and pours into his heart an indescribable joy, sweetness and peace even when he is in the midst of the most harrowing grief and suffering, as St Paul bears witness when he exclaims, "I exceedingly abound with joy in all our tribulations" (*2 Co* 7:4).[12]

Reflection

In completing these twelve days, we have begun our lifelong struggle to overcome the world. It is a battle we can win if we continue to fight and ask Our Lord and the Virgin Mary to sustain us. We have the help of the choirs of angels, our guardian angels and the Archangels, plus the intercession of all the wonderful saints of heaven.

> "We need saints to live in the world to sanctify the world and not to be afraid of living in the world, to taste the pure and nice things of the world, but who are not of the world." (Pope Francis)

Resolution

Blessed Mother, please help me not to be afraid of being the person God created me to be and help me rid myself of all the lies and deceits the world would have me believe. Help me to be inspired and guided by the gifts and fruits of the Holy Spirit. Help me not to be afraid of making mistakes or falling down, and to know that the greatest attribute of God's heart is his mercy and that he is a God who loves to forgive. Help me to stand up for the truth of Jesus in every situation and be a person who is firmly placed in the will of God and who trusts his love.

Recite the prayers for the day listed on page 92.

Days 13-19: Knowledge of Self

St Louis de Montfort describes the grace of self-knowledge as the "foundation of all other graces". Let us begin this next section with humility, asking Our Lady for the grace to see ourselves as we truly are, without condemnation but with conviction to change. We need her help to live the life of grace.

With an understanding of who we truly are comes an understanding of how much we need God. During this week we should bring to Our Lady any areas that the Holy Spirit reveals to us in our brokenness and sinfulness and ask Our Blessed Mother for the grace, through sacrifice and penance, to see ourselves as God sees us, to know ourselves as God knows us and to accept and love ourselves as God accepts and loves us.

Let us not be afraid during this week of self-knowledge to take Our Blessed Mother's hand (she was given to us at the feet of the crucified) and to go back into the past and face the monsters of our sins and failings.

All spiritual growth depends on our honesty with God and ourselves. It is only by the grace of God and through the gaze of Mary that we can be truly honest and have nothing to fear. To this end, during this week we will pray the Litany of the Holy Spirit, asking the Holy Spirit to illuminate our hearts to all the areas of ourselves that we do not know.

Day 13: Knowledge of Self

Theme: Through baptism we have been buried with
Christ so that we may be brought to life with him

Opening Prayer

Come Holy Spirit, come by means of the powerful
intercession of the Immaculate Heart of Mary your
well-beloved spouse. (*3 times*)

Scripture

Jesus said, 'Two men went up to the Temple to pray, one
a Pharisee, the other a tax collector. The Pharisee stood
there and said this prayer to himself, "I thank you, God,
that I am not grasping, unjust, adulterous like the rest
of mankind, and particularly that I am not like this tax
collector here. I fast twice a week; I pay tithes on all I
get." The tax collector stood some distance away, not
daring even to raise his eyes to heaven; but he beat his
breast and said, "God, be merciful to me, a sinner." This
man, I tell you, went home again at rights with God;
the other did not. For everyone who exalts himself will
be humbled, but the man who humbles himself will be
exalted.' (*Lk* 18:10-14)

Reading from St Louis de Montfort

"Men," says St Thomas, "vow in baptism to renounce
the devil and all his seductions." "This vow," says St

Augustine "is the greatest and the most indispensable of all vows." Canon Law experts say the same thing: "The vow we make at baptism is the most important of all vows." But does anyone keep this great vow? Does anyone fulfil the promises of baptism faithfully?

Is it not true that nearly all Christians prove unfaithful to the promises made to Jesus in baptism? Where does this universal failure come from, if not from man's habitual forgetfulness of the promises and responsibilities of baptism and from the fact that scarcely anyone makes a personal ratification of the contract made with God through his sponsors?[13]

Reflection

There are many areas of our past that we are scared to look at to see the true causes of our failures. Part of the freedom that God wants us to taste in our life is self-acceptance and understanding, and the only way we can come to this freedom is by looking at our past sins with the aid of the Holy Spirit and letting him show us their cause. Sometimes this can be painful, but our Blessed Mother is here to help us through this pain. The more we open the doors to all the areas of our lives to the light of the Holy Spirit and are not afraid to visit these memories, the freer we become.

St Teresa of Avila in her writings on the interior castle concludes that not to know and understand ourselves is folly, but true self-knowledge is the beginning of wisdom.

Resolution

Ask Our Lady for the grace to see our sinfulness without fear or condemnation, in the light of God's mercy.

Recite the prayers for the day listed on page 92.

DAY 14: Knowledge of Self

Theme: **Learning to be thankful; we are often ungrateful for what God has done for us**

Opening Prayer

Come Holy Spirit, come by means of the powerful intercession of the Immaculate Heart of Mary your well-beloved spouse. (*3 times*)

Scripture

Now on the way to Jerusalem he travelled along the border between Samaria and Galilee. As he entered one of the villages, ten lepers came to meet him. They stood some way off and called to him, 'Jesus! Master! Take pity on us.' When he saw them he said, 'Go and show yourselves to the priests.' Now as they were going away they were cleansed. Finding himself cured, one of them turned back praising God at the top of his voice and threw himself at the feet of Jesus and thanked him. The man was a Samaritan. This made Jesus say, 'Were not all ten made clean? The other nine, where are they? It seems that no one has come back to give praise to God, except this foreigner.' And he said to the man, 'Stand up and go on your way. Your faith has saved you.' (*Lk* 17:11-19)

Reading from St Louis de Montfort

To thank God for the graces he has given to Our Lady, her consecrated ones will frequently say the *Magnificat*, following the example of Blessed Marie d'Oignies and several other saints. The *Magnificat* is the only prayer we have which was composed by Our Lady, or rather, composed by Jesus in her, for it was he who spoke through her lips. It is the greatest offering of praise that God ever received under the law of grace. On the one hand, it is the most humble hymn of thanksgiving, and on the other, it is the most sublime and exalted. Contained in it are mysteries so great and so hidden that even the angels do not understand them.[14]

Reflection

In the book *From Prison to Praise* we learn that there is an incredible grace and power given to us when we are willing to thank and praise God for all that he gives us. It is often very easy and almost second nature to thank God when everything is going well, but how often do we thank God for everything: the good, the bad and the downright terrible? For when we learn to do this, in even the bad and the terrible, we will always see the love and reassurance of Jesus being with us. Sometimes this can be only a little glimpse, but nonetheless he is always there, and in these times we remember his words "I am with you always, even to the end of time". So let us never tire of thanking God, as we have a God who never tires of loving us.

St Augustine says the only thing we can do that is a completely selfless act towards God is to thank him and praise him for his goodness.

Resolution

Ask the Blessed Virgin Mary to inspire you to praise and thank God from your heart.

Recite the prayers for the day listed on page 92.

Day 15 - Knowledge of Self

Theme: Learning to live in the light and to be honest with ourselves

Opening Prayer

Come Holy Spirit, come by means of the powerful intercession of the Immaculate Heart of Mary your well-beloved spouse. (*3 times*)

Scripture

If we say that we are in union with God while we are living in darkness, we are lying because we are not living the truth. But if we live our lives in the light, as he is in the light, we are in union with one another, and the blood of Jesus, his Son, purifies us from all sin. If we say we have no sin in us, we are deceiving ourselves and refusing to admit the truth; but if we acknowledge our sins, then God who is faithful and just will forgive our sins and purify us from everything that is wrong. (*1 Jn* 1:6-10)

Reading from St Louis de Montfort

I admit that to be truly devoted to Our Lady, it is not absolutely necessary to be so holy as to avoid all sin, although this is desirable. But at least it is necessary (note what I am going to say), (1) to be genuinely determined to avoid at least all mortal sin, which outrages the

Mother as well as the Son; (2) to practise self-restraint in order to avoid sin; (3) to join her confraternities, say the Rosary and other prayers, fast on Saturdays, and so on.

Such means are surprisingly effective in converting even the hardened sinner. Should you be such a sinner, with one foot in the abyss, I advise you to do as I have said. But there is an essential condition. You must perform these good works solely to obtain from God, through the intercession of Our Lady, the grace to regret your sins, obtain pardon for them and overcome your evil habits, and not to live complacently in the state of sin, disregarding the warning voice of conscience, the example of Our Lord and the saints, and the teaching of the Holy Gospel.[15]

Reflection

Often we deceive ourselves about the real motivations for our actions, and it is only when we step back and have the honesty to invite the Holy Spirit and his wisdom into these situations that we see what our true motivation is. So let us during this week of self-knowledge make a commitment not to deceive ourselves, particularly about how easy it is to walk into occasions of sin, and to protect ourselves with truth and honesty. As one priest explained, if you are on a diet you should not work in a chocolate factory.

"All spiritual growth depends on honesty with ourselves and with God."
(Servant of God Fr Denis Herlihy)

Question

What sins in my life will I try and uproot with the help of God and his grace?

Resolution

Turn to the Rosary and ask Our Lady for the grace of transparency and honesty.

Recite the prayers for the day listed on page 92.

DAY 16: Knowledge of Self

Theme: Being changed from the inside out

Opening Prayer

Come Holy Spirit, come by means of the powerful intercession of the Immaculate Heart of Mary your well-beloved spouse. (*3 times*)

Scripture

Jesus said, "No one sews a piece of unshrunken cloth on an old cloak; if he does, the patch pulls away from it, the new from the old, and the tear gets worse. And nobody puts new wine into old wineskins; if he does, the wine will burst the skins, and the wine is lost and the skins too. No! New wine, fresh skins!' (*Mk* 2:21-22)

Reading from St Louis de Montfort

Our best actions are usually tainted and spoiled by the evil that is rooted in us. When pure, clear water is poured into a foul-smelling jug, or wine into an unwashed cask that previously contained another wine, the clear water and the good wine are tainted and readily acquire an unpleasant odour. In the same way when God pours into our soul, infected by original and actual sin, the heavenly waters of his grace or the delicious wines of his love, his gifts are usually spoiled and tainted by the evil sediment left in us by sin.[16]

Reflection

We inevitably make mistakes and fall down in the pursuit of loving and serving God, and often we hurt God much more by not getting up straight away from our failures and throwing ourselves into God's arms of mercy and forgiveness, as the prodigal son threw himself into his father's arms. Let us never forget that when we give God permission and invite him into our sinful nature, he is the person who heals and changes us. Not my will be done, but his will be done. Jesus said of St Mary Magdalen, those who are forgiven much, will love much.

St Thérèse of Lisieux said, "If I woke up having committed every mortal sin it was possible to commit I would have no other recourse but to throw myself into the arms of God my loving father and it would be like a drop of water falling into a roaring volcano."

Resolution

Let us ask Our Lady for the grace to begin anew each day and never be discouraged by our failures, but to see the hope that God's call holds for us.

Recite the prayers for the day listed on page 92.

DAY 17: Knowledge of Self

Theme: **Being carriers of God's grace**

Opening Prayer

Come Holy Spirit, come by means of the powerful intercession of the Immaculate Heart of Mary your well-beloved spouse. (*3 times*)

Scripture

The fact is, I know of nothing good living in me - living, that is, in my unspiritual self - for though the will to do what is good is in me, the performance is not, with the result that instead of doing the good things I want to do, I carry out the sinful things I do not want. When I act against my will, then, it is not my true self doing it, but sin which lives in me. (*Rm* 7:18-20)

Reading from St Louis de Montfort

It is very difficult, considering our weakness and frailty, to keep the graces and treasures we have received from God. We carry this treasure (his grace), which is worth more than heaven and earth, in fragile vessels, that is, in a corruptible body and in a weak and wavering soul which requires very little to depress and disturb it.[17]

Reflection

If we wait until we are perfect to serve God, we will never serve him because we will never be perfect. There was a man who felt he was always saying the wrong thing when speaking to people, so he decided to stop speaking. This went on for a whole week. A friend of his asked him why he was silent all the time. He explained his reason for this. The friend told him how foolish this was: "God has made you an outgoing, chatty person and he is using you in this way to touch many hearts."

We should not be afraid of making mistakes; we should be more afraid of not serving God in the freedom of our personalities.

"The glory of God is man fully alive." (St Irenaeus)

Questions

How do we treat the graces we have been given? Are they treated as the treasures they are, or do we not use them for fear of not doing it perfectly?

Resolution

Ask Our Lady for the grace to be good stewards of our personality and the gifts that have been bestowed upon us and not to be afraid to use them.

Recite the prayers for the day listed on page 92.

Day 18: Knowledge of Self

Theme: Being small in the eyes of God

Opening Prayer

Come Holy Spirit, come by means of the powerful intercession of the Immaculate Heart of Mary your well-beloved spouse. (*3 times*)

Scripture

Jesus said, 'I tell you solemnly, unless you change and become like little children you will never enter the kingdom of heaven. And so, the one who makes himself as little as this little child is the greatest in the kingdom of heaven'. (*Mt* 18:2-4)

Reading from St Louis de Montfort

In going to Jesus through Mary, we are really paying honour to Our Lord, for we are showing that, because of our sins, we are unworthy to approach his infinite holiness directly on our own. We are showing that we need Mary, his holy Mother, to be our advocate and mediatrix with him who is our Mediator. We are going to Jesus as Mediator and Brother, and at the same time humbling ourselves before him who is our God and our Judge. In short, we are practising humility, something that always gladdens the heart of God.[18]

Reflection

Betty Brennan has given many talks around the world to hundreds of thousands of people. She says that, before she speaks, she gives her pride, her wanting people to love and accept her, to God and asks him to use her in humility and smallness to glorify him. When we give God our pride and are willing to look at our pride, he gives us his humility and an understanding of what it is to be humble.

> "Satan can even clothe himself in a cloak of humility, but he does not know how to wear the cloak of obedience." (St Faustina)

Resolution

Blessed Mother, please help me to have humility and obedience to God's will in my life. Help me to wear the cloak of humility and obedience as you wore it.

Recite the prayers for the day listed on page 92.

DAY 19: Knowledge of Self

Theme: **Dying to our own will and being alive to God's plan**

Opening Prayer

Come Holy Spirit, come by means of the powerful intercession of the Immaculate Heart of Mary your well-beloved spouse. (*3 times*)

Scripture

Jesus said, 'I tell you, most solemnly, unless a wheat grain falls on the ground and dies, it remains only a single grain; but if it dies, it yields a rich harvest. Anyone who loves his life loses it; anyone who hates his life in this world will keep it for eternal life.' (*Jn* 12:24-25)

Reading from St Louis de Montfort

In order to empty ourselves of ourselves, we must die to ourselves daily. That is to say, we must renounce the operations of the powers of our soul, and of the senses of our body. We must see as if we saw not, understand as if we understood not, and make use of the things of this world as if we made no use of them at all. This is what St Paul calls dying daily; if the grain of corn falling on the earth does not die, it remains earth, and brings forth no good fruit. If we die not to ourselves, and if our holiest devotions do not incline us to this necessary and useful death, we shall bring forth no fruit worth anything, and our devotions will become useless. All our works will be stained by self-love and our own will; and this will cause God to hold in abomination the greatest sacrifices we can make, and the best actions we can do; so that at our death we shall find our hands empty of virtues and of merits, and we shall not have one spark of pure love, which is only communicated to souls dead to themselves, souls whose life is hidden with Jesus Christ in God.[19]

Reflection

We often hear people say, "What do you want to do when you grow up?" or "Have you thought about what you are going to do with your life?" What we should be saying is, "What does God want me to do with my life or how best can I seek his will?" True knowledge of self helps us to understand how much we need God, and knowing how much we need God helps us to understand how essential his will is in our lives. Let us live our lives according to his plan, knowing that our true happiness and freedom depend completely on this.

"Because God has made us for himself, our hearts are restless until they rest in him." (St Augustine)

Question

To die to oneself is not just to renounce sin but to purify our hearts. This change is not possible without the cross. Where do you encounter the cross in your life? Do you embrace the cross and try to carry it faithfully or do you seek out opportunities to set it aside?

Resolution

Ask Our Lady for the grace to see that in dying to ourselves we are giving up things that will not satisfy, in exchange for the good things God has planned for our happiness and fulfilment.

Recite the prayers for the day listed on page 92.

Now that you have completed these days of knowledge of self, take some time to reflect upon how sin enslaves us and keeps us from knowing the freedom for which we were created. In this reflection let us look at ways to be more open to God's will and obedient to that will, letting go of the world's lies and embracing God's truth.

Days 20-26: Knowledge of Mary

Spouse of the Spirit

Knowledge of Mary is a gift so great that it is nothing less than a privileged grace that one receives from the hand of the Almighty himself. St Louis de Montfort places a great emphasis on this in speaking of Our Lady:

"Mary is the supreme masterpiece of Almighty God and he has reserved the knowledge and possession of her for himself. Mary is the sealed fountain and the faithful spouse of the Holy Spirit, where only he may enter. She is the sanctuary and resting-place of the Blessed Trinity where God dwells in greater and more divine splendour than anywhere else in the universe, not excluding his dwelling above the cherubim and seraphim. No creature, however pure, may enter there without being specially privileged."[20]

Our Lady is inviting us to go deeper into a more personal and intimate relationship with her that will lead us into the heart of Christ her Son. To that end, this week we will pray the Litany of the Blessed Virgin Mary, asking for the grace of a deeper knowledge of her role.

It is recommended that you pray a Rosary each day, throughout the rest of the consecration.

DAY 20: Knowledge of Mary

Theme: **Our Lady is the carrier of God's grace to us**

Opening Prayer

Come Holy Spirit, come by means of the powerful intercession of the Immaculate Heart of Mary your well-beloved spouse. (*3 times*)

Scripture

Now a great sign appeared in heaven: a woman, adorned with the sun, standing on the moon, and with twelve stars on her head for a crown. (*Rv* 12:1)

Reading from St Louis de Montfort

Mary alone found grace before God without the help of any other creature. All those who have since found grace before God have found it only through her. She was full of grace when she was greeted by the Archangel Gabriel and was filled with grace to overflowing by the Holy Spirit when he so mysteriously overshadowed her. From day to day, from moment to moment, she increased so much this twofold plenitude that she attained an immense and inconceivable degree of grace. So much so, that the Almighty made her the sole custodian of his treasures and the sole dispenser of his graces. She can now ennoble, exalt and enrich all she chooses. She can lead them along the narrow path to heaven and guide them through the narrow gate to life. She can give a royal throne, sceptre and crown to whom she wishes. Jesus is always and everywhere the fruit and Son of Mary, and Mary is everywhere the genuine tree that bears that fruit of life, the true Mother who bears that Son.[21]

Reflection

A priest once mentioned that he was doing quite well and had a good relationship with Jesus, then a beautiful Lady came along and showed him oceans of Jesus that he never knew existed. That Lady was Mary, our Blessed Mother.

St Thérèse of Lisieux says there is an elevator that leads us directly to heaven, which many believe is the act of consecrating our heart to Jesus through Mary.

Resolution

Let us ask Mary to reveal Jesus to us, and in so doing reveal herself to us.

Recite the prayers for the day listed on page 92.

Day 21: Knowledge of Mary

Theme: **Our Lady as our defender from evil**

Opening Prayer

Come Holy Spirit, come by means of the powerful intercession of the Immaculate Heart of Mary your well-beloved spouse. (*3 times*)

Scripture

But the Lord God called to the man. 'Where are you?' he asked. 'I heard the sound of you in the garden,' he replied. 'I was afraid because I was naked, so I hid.' 'Who told you that you were naked?' he asked. 'Have you been eating of the tree I forbade you to eat?' The man replied, 'It was the woman you put with me; she gave me the fruit, and I ate it.' Then the Lord God asked the woman, 'What is this you have done?' The woman replied, 'The serpent tempted me and I ate.'

Then the Lord God said to the serpent, 'Because you have done this, be accursed beyond all cattle, all wild beasts. You shall crawl on your belly and eat dust every day of your life. I will make you enemies of each other: you and the woman, your offspring and her offspring. It will crush your head and you will strike its heel.' (*Gn* 3:10-15)

Reading from St Louis de Montfort
God has established only one enmity - but it is an irreconcilable one - which will last, and even go on increasing to the end of time. That enmity is between Mary, his worthy Mother, and the devil, between the children and the servants of the Blessed Virgin and the children and followers of Lucifer. Thus the most fearful enemy that God has set up against the devil is Mary, his holy Mother.[22]

Reflection
One night a person had a dream, and in that dream there was a man who was possessed by evil spirits. Having tried everything to set this man free, the person then said three times, "Come Holy Spirit, come by means of the powerful intercession of the Immaculate Heart of Mary your well-beloved spouse", at which the man was completely delivered. In our everyday life there is no greater weapon against evil than the gift of Mary through the grace of God.

"When we pray the rosary we chain up the devil." (Padre Pio)

Resolution
Ask the Blessed Virgin Mary for the grace of spiritual protection from any attacks or snares of the evil one.

Recite the prayers for the day listed on page 92.

Day 22: Knowledge of Mary

Theme: **Our Lady teaches us how to receive like children**

Opening Prayer

Come Holy Spirit, come by means of the powerful intercession of the Immaculate Heart of Mary your well-beloved spouse. (*3 times*)

Scripture

Jesus said 'Ask, and it will be given to you; search, and you will find; knock, and the door will be opened to you. For the one who asks always receives; the one who searches always finds; the one who knocks will always have the door opened to him. Is there a man among you who would hand his son a stone when he asked for bread? Or would hand him a snake when he asked for a fish? If you, then, who are evil, know how to give your children what is good, how much more will your Father in heaven give good things to those who ask him!' (*Mt 7:7-11*)

Reading from St Louis de Montfort

As in natural life a child must have a father and a mother, so in the supernatural life of grace a true child of the Church must have God for his Father and Mary for his mother. If anyone, then, wishes to become a member of Jesus Christ, and consequently be filled with grace and truth, he must be formed in Mary through the grace of Jesus Christ, which she possesses with a fullness enabling her to communicate it abundantly to true members of Jesus Christ, her true children.[23]

Reflection

Whenever we have a problem or a situation for which we can find no solution, if we take the time to talk about it to our Blessed mother, she seems to give us the answer, take away the problem and give us her peace.

"When Mary guides you, you will feel no fatigue." (St Bernard of Clairvaux)

Resolution

Ask Our Blessed Mother to open our hearts to her so that we may receive her peace like a child who trusts in its mother.

Recite the prayers for the day listed on page 92.

Day 23 - Knowledge of Mary

Theme: **Through Our Lady we find a deeper union with Christ**

Opening Prayer

Come Holy Spirit, come by means of the powerful intercession of the Immaculate Heart of Mary your well-beloved spouse. (*3 times*)

Scripture

While they were there the time came for her to have her child, and she gave birth to a son, her first-born. She wrapped him in swaddling clothes, and laid him in a manger because there was no room for them at the inn. (*Lk 2:6-7*)

Reading from St Louis de Montfort

Mary is the most perfect and the most holy of all creatures, and Jesus, who came to us in a perfect manner, chose no other road for his great and wonderful journey. The Most High, the Incomprehensible One, the Inaccessible One, he who is, deigned to come down to us poor earthly creatures who are nothing at all. How was this done? The Most High God came down to us in a perfect way through the humble Virgin Mary, without losing anything of his divinity or holiness. It is likewise through Mary that we poor creatures must ascend to almighty God in a perfect manner without having anything to fear. God the Incomprehensible allowed himself to be perfectly comprehended and contained by the humble Virgin Mary without losing anything of his immensity. So we must let ourselves be perfectly contained and led by the humble Virgin without any reserve on our part.

God the Inaccessible drew near to us and united himself closely, perfectly and even personally to our humanity through Mary without losing anything of his majesty. So it is also through Mary that we must draw near to God and unite ourselves to him perfectly, intimately, and without fear of being rejected. Lastly, he who is deigned to come down to us who are not, and turned our nothingness into God, or he who is. He did this perfectly by giving and submitting himself entirely to the young Virgin Mary, without ceasing to be in time he who is from all eternity. Likewise it is through Mary that we, who are nothing, may become like God by grace and glory. We accomplish this by giving ourselves to her so perfectly and so completely as to remain nothing, as far as self is concerned, and to be everything in her, without any fear of illusion.[24]

Reflection

There was once a soul living in a religious community, who often felt very unworthy to go directly to Jesus, but had no problem praying and speaking to our Blessed Mother and by doing this was brought back to unity with Jesus.

"When you know Mary, you know Jesus." (Blessed Mother Teresa)

Resolution

We ask Mary to hold us in our helplessness as she held the baby Jesus in his vulnerability.

Recite the prayers for the day listed on page 92.

Day 24: Knowledge of Mary

Theme: **We can trust Our Lady with all we have, both material and spiritual**

Opening Prayer

Come Holy Spirit, come by means of the powerful intercession of the Immaculate Heart of Mary your well-beloved spouse. (*3 times*)

Scripture

Jesus said 'Do not store up treasures for yourselves on earth, where moths and woodworms destroy them and thieves can break in and steal. But store up treasures for yourselves in heaven, where neither moths nor woodworms destroy them and thieves cannot break in and steal. For where your treasure is, there will your heart be also.' (*Mt* 6:19-21)

Reading from St Louis de Montfort

Rejoice and be glad! Here is a secret, which I am revealing to you, a secret unknown to most Christians, even the most devout. Do not commit the gold of your charity, the silver of your purity to a threadbare sack or a battered old chest, or the waters of heavenly grace or the wines of your merits and virtues to a tainted and fetid cask, such as you are. Otherwise you will be robbed by thieving devils that are on the lookout day and night waiting for a favourable opportunity to plunder. If you do so, all those pure gifts from God will be spoiled by the unwholesome presence of self-love, inordinate self-reliance, and self-will.

Pour into the bosom and the heart of Mary all your treasures, all your graces, and all your virtues. She is a spiritual vessel, she is a vessel of honour, and she is a marvellous vessel of devotion. Since God himself has been shut up in person, with all his perfections, in that vessel, it has become altogether spiritual, and the spiritual abode of the most spiritual souls. It has become honourable, and the throne of honour for the grandest princes of eternity. It has become wonderful in devotion, and a dwelling the most illustrious for sweetnesses, for graces, and for virtues. It has become rich as a house of gold, strong as a tower of David, and pure as a tower of ivory.[25]

Reflection

A woman was very worried about her teenage son, who seemed to be destroying himself with drugs and drink, so she consecrated him one day to the Immaculate Heart of Mary. After a short time the young man was converted and became a religious brother. He was asked to give his testimony at his local church and brought from the family home the picture of Mary he had prayed to in the lead up to his conversion. Coming back from the talk, he noticed his name was written on the back of the picture. He asked his mother why this was. She said, "When I consecrated you to the Heart of Mary I wrote your name on the back of the picture as a sign of your consecration."

"You only have to see how much God the Father trusted Mary with our salvation, Jesus as a helpless baby, to see how much we can trust Mary." (Fr Stephen Vooght)

Questions

What are the greatest blessings you have received? What is the most prized treasure of your heart? Now have the confidence to turn all of these over to the care and custody of Our Lady.

Resolution

Let us ask God for the grace to give everything to him through Mary.

Recite the prayers for the day listed on page 92.

Day 25: Knowledge of Mary

Theme: **Our Lady helps us to be simple**

Opening Prayer

Come Holy Spirit, come by means of the powerful intercession of the Immaculate Heart of Mary your well-beloved spouse. (*3 times*)

Scripture

People brought little children to him, for him to lay his hands on them and say a prayer. The disciples turned them away, but Jesus said, 'Let the little children alone, and do not stop them coming to me; for it is to such as these that the kingdom of heaven belongs.' (*Mt* 19:13-14)

Reading from St Louis de Montfort

To sum up, Mary becomes all things for the soul that wishes to serve Jesus Christ. She enlightens his mind with her pure faith. She deepens his heart with her humility. She enlarges and inflames his heart with her charity, makes it pure with her purity, makes it noble and great through her motherly care. But why dwell any longer on this? Experience alone will teach us the wonders wrought by Mary in the soul, wonders so great that the wise and the proud, and even a great number of devout people, find it hard to credit them.[26]

Reflection

A best-selling author, who had led a life of crime before he was converted, recalled how his mother wouldn't read the first half of his autobiography where he described his life as a gangster, but enjoyed reading the second half which described his growing in the wonder and love of God. When he was on his way to meet his mother, his brother rang him and told him their mother had now read the first half of the book. He was filled with trepidation at what she might think. When he asked her what she felt about all the terrible things he had done, she said, "I thought, 'My poor, wounded little boy!'" and started crying.

When we see ourselves through the eyes of our Blessed Mother we are never judged or condemned, but see ourselves through the merciful loving eyes of Christ.

"When you pray to Mary you will not despair" (St Bernard)

Questions

What aspect of your spirit is most like Our Lady? Which aspect is most unlike and opposed to her?

Resolution

Let us ask our Blessed Mother's help to see ourselves as she sees us.

Recite the prayers for the day listed on page 92.

Day 26: Knowledge of Mary

Theme: **Growing closer to Our Lady leads us into discipleship of Christ**

Opening Prayer

Come Holy Spirit, come by means of the powerful intercession of the Immaculate Heart of Mary your well-beloved spouse. (*3 times*)

Scripture

Jesus said 'The disciple is not superior to his teacher, nor the slave to his master. It is enough for the disciple that he should grow to be like his teacher, and the slave like his master.' (*Mt* 10:24-25)

Reading from St Louis de Montfort

St Augustine, speaking to our Blessed Lady, says, "You are worthy to be called the mould of God." Mary is a mould capable of forming people into the image of the God-man. Anyone who is cast into this divine mould is quickly shaped and moulded into Jesus and Jesus into him. At little cost and in a short time he will become Christ-like since he is cast into the very same mould that fashioned a God-man.[27]

Reflection

There was a young boy whose mother couldn't love him and ended up badly mistreating him, both physically and mentally. Many years later, when he was thirty-eight years old, he discovered his heavenly mother as he was praying a Rosary in a prayer house. Mary revealed to him the tenderness and love that he had never experienced before at the hands of his own mother. Three days later she took him to heaven as he was baptised on his deathbed, following a sudden brain haemorrhage.

"When we take the rosary, we take our Lady's hand and we are led to where Jesus wants us to be." (St Dominic)

Questions

Do we really believe that Jesus wants the best for us in our lives, and if we do, what is stopping us giving everything to Mary and in so doing receiving the very best from Jesus?

Resolution

In our Rosary let us ask Mary to reveal everything Jesus wants from us and for the grace to be able to surrender all those things to him.

Recite the prayers for the day listed on page 92.

Days 27-33: Knowledge of Jesus Christ

As we are seeking to know Jesus in a more personal and intimate way, this is the week where we enter into the person who is the beginning and the end, the alpha and the omega. First, we rid ourselves of all the worldly distractions that stop us realising the wonder of Jesus as our friend and saviour. Then we begin understanding our motivations and desires through the knowledge of ourselves, and get to grips with the essential reason for our being which is to love and understand God. We have then taken Mary's hand to be led into the heart of her son where we can be brought to the hidden life of Jesus through the eyes of our Blessed Mother. For if we want to know the Son, let us ask his Mother.

During this week we will come to know Jesus's humanity and his divinity, the humble God who comes in the form of bread so that we might draw life from him. For when we look at Jesus we see the creator of the universe and our personal friend who knows and loves us so deeply and completely. What a blessing and what a joy to know Jesus more and more and to understand his love, which is beyond all knowledge, and can only be revealed through the guidance and wisdom of the Holy Spirit and his spouse.

God our Father, open the eyes of our hearts that we might know Jesus your Son more fully and completely than ever before.

This week we will pray the Litany of the Sacred Heart, asking for the grace of a deeper union with Christ.

DAY 27: Knowledge of Jesus Christ

Theme: Christ is the pearl of great price, and without him we are never satisfied, fulfilled or complete.

Opening Prayer

Come Holy Spirit, come by means of the powerful intercession of the Immaculate Heart of Mary, your well-beloved spouse. (*3 times*)

Scripture

Jesus said, 'I am the true vine, and my Father is the vinedresser. Every branch in me that bears no fruit he cuts away, and every branch that does bear fruit he prunes to make it bear even more. You are pruned already, by means of the word that I have spoken to you. Make your home in me, as I make mine in you. As a branch cannot bear fruit all by itself, but must remain part of the vine, neither can you unless you remain in me. I am the vine, you are the branches. Whoever remains in me, with me in him, bears fruit in plenty; for cut off from me you can do nothing.' (*Jn* 15:1-5)

Reading from St Louis de Montfort

Jesus, our Saviour, true God and true man, must be the ultimate end of all our other devotions; otherwise they would be false and misleading. He is the Alpha and the Omega, the beginning and end of everything. "We labour," says St. Paul, "only to make all men perfect in Jesus Christ." For in him alone dwells the entire fullness of the divinity and the complete fullness of grace, virtue and perfection. In him alone we have been blessed with every spiritual blessing; he is the only teacher from whom we must learn; the only Lord on whom we should depend; the only Head to whom we should be united and the only model that we should imitate. He is the only Physician that can heal us; the only Shepherd that can feed us; the only Way that can lead us; the only Truth that we can believe; the only Life that can animate us. He alone is everything to us and he alone can satisfy all our desires.[28]

Reflection

There was an atheist who was in hospital, seriously ill. When an Irish Catholic nurse said to him, "You have had everything that the world can offer you but you have never been satisfied or fulfilled", he couldn't get these words out of his heart, as he had always felt there was something missing from his life. In the last months of his life he found a personal relationship with Jesus and realised that it was this that was missing. Each one of us has a heart that is restless until it rests in the loving arms of Jesus.

"There is a part of our heart that will never be satisfied or complete, no matter how rich or famous we become, until we are brought to a personal relationship with Jesus." (St John Paul II)

Resolution
Lord Jesus, help us to know you personally so we might have the freedom you created us for.

Recite the prayers for the day listed on page 92.

Day 28: Knowledge of Jesus Christ

Theme: In Jesus, God comes to us in his humanity

Opening Prayer

Come Holy Spirit, come by means of the powerful intercession of the Immaculate Heart of Mary your well-beloved spouse. (*3 times*)

Scripture

In the beginning was the Word: the Word was with God and the Word was God. He was with God in the beginning. Through him all things came to be; not one thing had its being but through him. All that came to be had life in him and that life was the light of men, a light that shines in the dark, a light that darkness could not overpower. The Word was the true light that enlightens all men; and he was coming into the world. The Word was made flesh, he lived among us, and we saw his glory, the glory that is his as the only Son of the Father, full of grace and truth. Indeed, from his fullness we have, all of us, received - yes, grace in return for grace. (*Jn* 1:1-5,9,14,16)

Reading from St Louis de Montfort

During her whole life, our Saviour's holy Mother was occupied in meditating on the virtues and the sufferings of her Son. When she heard the angels sing their hymn of joy at his birth and saw the shepherds adore him in the stable, her heart was filled with wonder and she meditated on all these marvels. She compared the greatness of the Word incarnate to the way he humbled himself in this lowly fashion; the straw of the crib, to his throne in the heart of his Father; the might of God, to the weakness of his simplicity.[29]

Reflection

A man who had just been converted, and who was filled with the Holy Spirit, wanted to evangelise. He said to his parish priest, "We need to go out and tell everyone about Jesus." The priest replied, "I have a curate who is a great preacher, and when he preaches many people come to know Jesus. At the moment he is doing the washing up, then he is going to vacuum the front room and tidy up the house. Know that Jesus is in the ordinary everyday things as well as the extraordinary." Jesus is in our humanity as he reveals his humanity.

"Jesus is in the pots and pans of everyday life." (St Teresa of Avila)

Resolution

Jesus, help us to understand that you are interested in the hidden small things of our life and help us to be honest and real with you.

Recite the prayers for the day listed on page 92.

Day 29: Knowledge of Jesus Christ

Theme: We cannot have humility without obedience

Opening Prayer

Come Holy Spirit, come by means of the powerful intercession of the Immaculate Heart of Mary your well-beloved spouse. (*3 times*)

Scripture

"Why were you looking for me?" he replied. "Did you not know that I must be busy with my Father's affairs?" But they did not understand what he meant. He then went down with them and came to Nazareth and lived under their authority. His mother stored up all these things in her heart. And Jesus increased in wisdom, in stature, and in favour with God and men. (*Lk* 2:49-52)

Reading from St Louis de Montfort

Our good Master stooped to enclose himself in the womb of the Blessed Virgin, a captive but loving slave, and to make himself subject to her for thirty years. As I said earlier, the human mind is bewildered when it reflects seriously upon this conduct of Incarnate Wisdom. He did not choose to give himself in a direct manner to the human race though he could easily have done so. He chose to come through the Virgin Mary.

What immeasurable glory then do we give to God when, following the example of Jesus, we submit to Mary! With such a convincing and well-known example before us, can we be so foolish as to believe that there is a better and shorter way of giving God glory than by submitting ourselves to Mary, as Jesus did?[30]

Reflection

A person who was in a religious community was struggling with the people who God had put in charge of him, and on one occasion was telling someone how weak and broken his superiors were. The person listened very attentively to his story, and then said to him "What do they think of you?" It is very easy for us to work out all the reasons why we shouldn't be obedient, instead of showing the humility of Jesus, who was obedient even unto death.

"Obedience is infallible when it is not contrary to morality" (Blessed Mother Teresa)

Question

How obedient am I? Am I willing to follow and learn from Mary as Jesus did?

Resolution

Lord Jesus, help us to have the humility and obedience that you have showed us through your witness.

Recite the prayers for the day listed on page 92.

Day 30: Knowledge of Jesus Christ

Theme: Take up your cross and follow me

Opening Prayer

Come Holy Spirit, come by means of the powerful intercession of the Immaculate Heart of Mary your well-beloved spouse. (*3 times*)

Scripture

The passers-by jeered at him; they shook their heads and said, 'So you would destroy the Temple and rebuild it in three days! Then save yourself! If you are God's son, come down from the cross!' The chief priests with the scribes and elders mocked him in the same way. 'He saved others;' they said 'he cannot save himself. He is the king of Israel; let him come down from the cross now, and we will believe in him.' (*Mt* 27:38-44)

Reading from St Louis de Montfort

Incarnate Wisdom loved the cross from his infancy (*Ws* 8:2). At his coming into the world, while in his Mother's womb, he received it from his eternal Father. He placed it deep in his heart, there to dominate his life, saying, "My God and my Father, I chose this cross when I was in your bosom (*Ps* 39:9). I choose it now in the womb of my Mother. I love it with all my strength and I place it deep in my heart to be my spouse and my mistress."[31]

Reflection

During his prayers a pilgrim was complaining to Jesus about his cross being too heavy and burdensome. Jesus appeared to him and showed him a door. He opened the door, and saw a room filled with different-sized crosses. Jesus said, "Take your pick". The pilgrim selected his ideal cross and went on his way. As the man examined his cross again, he realised he had chosen the exact same cross he had been complaining about. God never gives us a burden too heavy for us to carry, because it is with his help and grace that we carry that burden.

> "Behold the cross of the Lord; when all adversity surrounds you, rejoice, for the Lion of Judah has conquered!" (St Anthony of Padua)

Resolution

Lord Jesus, help us to carry our crosses in life, as you carried our crosses to your death.

Recite the prayers for the day listed on page 92.

Day 31: Knowledge of Jesus Christ

Theme: No one can have greater love than to lay down his life for his friends.

Opening Prayer

Come Holy Spirit, come by means of the powerful intercession of the Immaculate Heart of Mary your well-beloved spouse. (*3 times*)

Scripture

Jesus said, 'As the Father has loved me, so I have loved you. Remain in my love. If you keep my commandments you will remain in my love, just as I have kept my Father's commandments and remain in his love. I have told you this so that my own joy may be in you and your joy be complete. This is my commandment: love one another, as I have loved you. A man can have no greater love than to lay down his life for his friends.' (*Jn* 15:9-13)

Reading from St Louis de Montfort

The Holy Spirit tells us, through the Apostles, to contemplate the crucified Christ. He bids us arm ourselves with this thought, for it is the most powerful and formidable weapon against our enemies. When you are assailed by poverty, disrepute, sorrow, temptation, and other crosses, arm yourselves with the shield, breastplate, helmet and two-edged sword, which is the remembrance of Christ crucified. It is there you will find the solution of every problem and the means to conquer all your enemies.[32]

Reflection

Many people look at the cross and see their salvation, but do not see the humble figure of Mary with her hand stretched out to us, asking us to take her hand and journey through that crucifixion to the resurrection that Christ's death brought each one of us. Once, a person was very impressed with a woman filled with the grace of God, and said to her "I want your peace." She replied, "Are you willing to be crucified to receive it?"

> "The devil's greatest tactic is to hide the true meaning of the cross from us." (Archbishop Fulton Sheen)

Resolution

Mary, help us take you by the hand; lead us through the crucifixion where we will find the freedom that Christ's death brought each one of us.

Recite the prayers for the day listed on page 92.

Day 32 - Knowledge of Jesus Christ

Theme: The Blessed Sacrament is the source and summit of our faith.

Opening Prayer

Come Holy Spirit, come by means of the Immaculate Heart of Mary, your well-beloved spouse. (3 times)

Scripture

Then he took some bread, and when he had given thanks, broke it and gave it to them, saying, 'This is my body which will be given for you; do this as a memorial of me.' He did the same with the cup after supper, and said, 'This cup is the new covenant in my blood which will be poured out for you.' (*Lk* 22:19-20)

Reading from St Louis de Montfort

Eternal Wisdom, on the one hand, wished to prove his love for man by dying in his place in order to save him, but on the other hand, he could not bear the thought of leaving him. So he devised a marvellous way of dying and living at the same time, and of abiding with man until the end of time. So, in order fully to satisfy his love, he instituted the sacrament of Holy Eucharist and went to the extent of changing and overturning nature itself.

He does not conceal himself under a sparkling diamond or some other precious stone, because he does not want to abide with man in an ostentatious manner. But he hides himself under the appearance of a small piece of bread - man's ordinary nourishment - so that when received he might enter the heart of man and there take his delight. *Ardenter amantium hoc est* - Those who love ardently act in this way. "O eternal Wisdom," says a saint, "O God who is truly lavish with himself in his desire to be with man."[33]

Reflection

A famous author's son wrote to him saying he was feeling hopelessness and despair and feared he was losing his faith. His father replied, "If there is one thing to put in the centre of your life so that you will always have fulfilment and deep faith in God, it is the Eucharist". When we start going to Mass daily and spending time with Jesus in the Blessed Sacrament in adoration, our lives are transformed, for we place ourselves in the miracles of our humble God who comes in the form of bread that we may draw life from him.

"All my strength comes from one source, Jesus in the Eucharist." (Blessed Mother Teresa)

"It would be easier for the earth to exist without the sun than without the Holy Mass." (Padre Pio)

Resolution

Lord Jesus, give me eyes that I might see the glory of you made present in the form of bread

Recite the prayers for the day listed on page 92.

Day 33: Knowledge of Jesus Christ

Theme: **To know Jesus is to serve him and to do his will**

Opening Prayer

Come Holy Spirit, come by means of the powerful intercession of the Immaculate Heart of Mary your well-beloved spouse. (*3 times*)

Scripture

Lastly, Jesus showed himself to the Eleven themselves while they were at table. He reproached them for their incredulity and obstinacy, because they had refused to believe those who had seen him after he had risen. And he said to them, 'Go out to the whole world; proclaim the Good News to all creation. He who believes and is baptised will be saved; he who does not believe will be condemned. These are the signs that will be associated with believers: in my name they will cast out devils; they will have the gift of tongues; they will pick up snakes in their hands, and be unharmed should they drink deadly poison; they will lay their hands on the sick, who will recover.' (*Mk* 16:14-18)

Reading from St Louis de Montfort

But what will they be like, these servants, these slaves, these children of Mary?

They will be ministers of the Lord who, like a flaming fire, will enkindle everywhere the fires of divine love. They will become, in Mary's powerful hands, like sharp arrows, with which she will transfix her enemies. They will be as the children of Levi, thoroughly purified by the fire of great tribulations and closely joined to God. They will carry the gold of love in their heart, the frankincense of prayer in their mind and the myrrh of mortification in their body. They will bring to the poor and lowly everywhere the sweet fragrance of Jesus, but they will bring the odour of death to the great, the rich and the proud of this world.

They will be like thunderclouds flying through the air at the slightest breath of the Holy Spirit. Attached to nothing, surprised at nothing, troubled by nothing, they will shower down the rain of God's word and of eternal life. They will thunder against sin, they will storm against the world, they will strike down the devil and his followers and for life and for death, they will pierce through and through with the two-edged sword of God's word all those against whom they are sent by Almighty God.

They will be true apostles of the latter times to whom the Lord of Hosts will give eloquence and strength to work wonders and carry off glorious spoils from his enemies. They will sleep without gold or silver and, more important still, without concern in the midst of other priests, ecclesiastics and clerics. Yet they will have the silver wings of the dove enabling them to go wherever the Holy Spirit calls them, filled as they are with the resolve to seek the glory of God and the salvation of souls. Wherever they preach, they will leave behind them nothing but the gold of love, which is the fulfilment of the whole law.

Lastly, we know they will be true disciples of Jesus Christ, imitating his poverty, his humility, his contempt for the world, and his love. They will point out the narrow way to God in pure truth according to the holy Gospel, and not according to the maxims of the world. Their hearts will not be troubled, nor will they show favour to anyone; they will not spare or heed or fear any man, however powerful he may be. They will have the two-edged sword of the word of God in their mouths and the bloodstained standard of the Cross on their shoulders. They will carry the crucifix in their right hand and the rosary in their left, and the holy names of Jesus and Mary on their heart. The simplicity and self-sacrifice of Jesus will be reflected in their whole behaviour.

Such are the great men who are to come. By the will of God, Mary is to prepare them to extend his rule over the impious and unbelievers. But when and how will this come about? Only God knows. For our part we must yearn and wait for it in silence and in prayer: "I have waited and waited."[34]

Reflection

When we consecrate our heart to Jesus through Mary, we take on a role, which is to bring the love of Christ to all who we meet. We step out in faith with a resolute commitment to bring others to a deep knowledge of the role of Mary and an understanding of everyone's need of Jesus. Let us not be afraid to stand up for Christ in all that we do and all we are, through the way we live and the way we speak, bringing his truth to a world that is in desperate need of it. A wise old man once asked a young boy, "What is the most important thing in life?" The boy replied, "You are much older and wiser than me; what is it?" The old man said, "To bring as many souls to God as possible and your own first!"

"Do not be afraid to proclaim the Gospel from the rooftops!" (St John Paul II)

Resolution

Let us ask our Blessed Mother to help us make a resolution and a promise to try to be fearless witnesses of the light of Christ, through going to confession regularly, receiving Jesus in the Blessed Sacrament as often as possible, by praying the rosary daily and receiving all the graces we need to truly serve her son Jesus Christ, our Lord and God, by being obedient to his will.

Recite the prayers for the day listed on page 92.

Prayers

Each section of the consecration has specific prayers to be prayed each day. These are all listed below.

Prayers for days 1-12: Renouncing the Spirit of the World for the Spirit of the Gospel
Veni Creator, Ave Maris Stella, Magnificat.

Prayers for days 13-19: Knowledge of Self
Veni Creator, Ave Maris Stella, Magnificat, Litany of the Holy Spirit.

Prayers for days 20-26: Knowledge of Mary
Veni Creator, Ave Maris Stella, Magnificat, Litany of the Blessed Virgin Mary, St Louis de Montfort's prayer to Mary.

Prayers for days 27-33: Knowledge of Jesus Christ
Veni Creator, Ave Maris Stella, Magnificat, Litany of the Sacred Heart, St Louis de Montfort's prayer to Jesus.

Veni Creator

Come, O Creator Spirit blest!
And in our souls take up your rest;
Come with your grace and heavenly aid,
To fill the hearts which you have made.

Great Comforter! To you we cry,
O highest gift of God Most High!
O Fount of Life! O Fire of Love!
And sweet anointing from above.

You in your many gifts are known,
The finger of God's hand we own;
The promise of the Father, thou!
Who does the tongue with power endow.

Kindle our senses from above,
And make our hearts overflow with love;
With patience firm and virtue high,
The weakness of our flesh supply.

Drive far from us the foe we dread,
And grant us your true peace instead;
So shall we not, with you for guide,
Turn from the path of life aside.

O may your grace on us bestow
The Father and the Son to know,
And evermore to hold confessed
Yourself of each the Spirit blest.

All glory while the ages run
Be to the Father and the Son
Who rose from death; the same to thee,
O Holy Ghost, eternally. Amen.

Ave Maris Stella
Hail, bright star of ocean,
God's own Mother blest,
Ever-sinless Virgin,
Gate of heavenly rest.

Taking that sweet Ave
Which from Gabriel came,
Peace confirm within us,
Changing Eva's name.

Break the captives' fetters,
Light on blindness pour,
All our ills expelling,
Every bliss implore.

Show thyself a Mother;
May the Word Divine,
Born for us thy Infant,
Hear our prayers through thine.

Virgin all excelling,
Mildest of the mild,
Freed from guilt, preserve us,
Pure and undefiled.

Keep our life all spotless,
Make our way secure,
Till we find in Jesus,
Joy for evermore.

Through the highest heaven
To the Almighty Three,
Father, Son and Spirit,
One same glory be. Amen.

Magnificat
My soul glorifies the Lord,
my spirit rejoices in God, my Saviour.
He looks on his servant in her lowliness;
henceforth all ages will call me blessed.

The Almighty works marvels for me.
Holy his name!
His mercy is from age to age,
on those who fear him.

He puts forth his arm in strength
and scatters the proud-hearted.
He casts the mighty from their thrones
and raises the lowly.

He fills the starving with good things,
sends the rich away empty.

He protects Israel, his servant,
remembering his mercy,
the mercy promised to our fathers,
to Abraham and his sons forever.

Glory be to the Father and to the Son and to the Holy
Spirit, as it was in the beginning, is now, and ever shall
be, world without end. Amen.

Litany of the Holy Spirit

Lord, have mercy
Lord, have mercy
Christ, have mercy
Christ, have mercy
Lord, have mercy
Lord, have mercy
Father all powerful,
have mercy on us
Jesus, Eternal Son of the Father,
Redeemer of the world,
save us
Spirit of the Father and the Son,
boundless life of both,
sanctify us

Holy Trinity,
hear us
Holy Spirit, who proceeds from the Father and the Son,
enter our hearts
Holy Spirit, who is equal to the Father and the Son,
enter our hearts
Promise of God the Father,
have mercy on us
Ray of heavenly light,
have mercy on us
Author of all good,
have mercy on us

Source of heavenly water,
have mercy on us
Consuming fire,
have mercy on us
Ardent charity,
have mercy on us
Spiritual unction,
have mercy on us
Spirit of love and truth,
have mercy on us
Spirit of wisdom and
understanding,
have mercy on us
Spirit of counsel
and fortitude,
have mercy on us
Spirit of knowledge
and piety,
have mercy on us
Spirit of the fear of
the Lord,
have mercy on us
Spirit of grace and prayer,
have mercy on us

Spirit of peace and
meekness,
have mercy on us
Spirit of modesty
and innocence,
have mercy on us
Holy Spirit,
the Comforter,
have mercy on us
Holy Spirit, the Sanctifier,
have mercy on us
Holy Spirit, who governs
the Church,
have mercy on us
Gift of God
the Most High,
have mercy on us
Spirit who fills
the universe,
have mercy on us
Spirit of the adoption of
the children of God,
have mercy on us
Holy Spirit,
*inspire us with horror
of sin*

Holy Spirit,
*come and renew
the face of the earth*
Holy Spirit,
shed your light in our souls
Holy Spirit,
*engrave your law
in our hearts*
Holy Spirit,
*enflame us with the flame
of your love*
Holy Spirit,
*open to us the treasures
of your graces*
Holy Spirit,
teach us to pray well
Holy Spirit,
*enlighten us with your
heavenly inspirations*
Holy Spirit,
*lead us in the way
of salvation*
Holy Spirit,
*grant us the only
necessary knowledge*

Holy Spirit,
*inspire in us the practice
of good*
Holy Spirit,
*grant us the merits of all
virtues*
Holy Spirit,
make us persevere in justice
Holy Spirit,
be our everlasting reward
Lamb of God, who takes
away the sins of the world,
send us your Holy Spirit
Lamb of God, who takes
away the sins of the world,
*pour down into our souls
the gifts of the Holy Spirit*
Lamb of God, who takes
away the sins of the world,
*grant us the Spirit of
wisdom and piety*
Come, Holy Spirit, fill the
hearts of your faithful,
*and enkindle in them the
fire of your love*

Let us pray

Grant, O merciful Father, that your Divine Spirit may enlighten, inflame and purify us, that he may penetrate us with his heavenly dew and make us fruitful in good works, through Our Lord Jesus Christ, your Son, who with you, in the unity of the same Spirit, lives and reigns, one God, forever and ever. Amen.

Litany of the Blessed Virgin Mary

Lord have mercy
Lord have mercy
Christ have mercy
Christ have mercy
Lord have mercy
Lord have mercy
Christ, hear us
Christ, graciously hear us
God the Father
of Heaven,
have mercy on us
God the Son,
Redeemer of the world,
have mercy on us
God the Holy Spirit,
have mercy on us

Holy Trinity, one God,
have mercy on us
Holy Mary,
pray for us
Holy Mother of God,
pray for us
Holy Virgin of virgins,
pray for us
Mother of Christ,
pray for us
Mother of divine grace,
pray for us
Mother most pure,
pray for us
Mother most chaste,
pray for us

Mother inviolate,
pray for us
Mother undefiled,
pray for us
Mother most amiable,
pray for us
Mother most admirable,
pray for us
Mother of good counsel,
pray for us
Mother of our Creator,
pray for us
Mother of our Redeemer,
pray for us
Virgin most prudent,
pray for us
Virgin most venerable,
pray for us
Virgin most renowned,
pray for us
Virgin most powerful,
pray for us
Virgin most merciful,
pray for us

Virgin most faithful,
pray for us
Mirror of justice,
pray for us
Seat of wisdom,
pray for us
Cause of our joy,
pray for us
Spiritual vessel,
pray for us
Vessel of honour,
pray for us
Singular vessel of
devotion,
pray for us
Mystical rose,
pray for us
Tower of David,
pray for us
Tower of ivory,
pray for us
House of gold,
pray for us
Ark of the covenant,
pray for us

Gate of Heaven,
pray for us
Morning Star,
pray for us
Health of the sick,
pray for us
Refuge of sinners,
pray for us
Comforter of the afflicted,
pray for us
Help of Christians,
pray for us
Queen of Angels,
pray for us
Queen of Patriarchs,
pray for us
Queen of Prophets,
pray for us
Queen of Apostles,
pray for us
Queen of Martyrs,
pray for us
Queen of Confessors,
pray for us
Queen of Virgins,
pray for us

Queen of all Saints,
pray for us
Queen conceived
without original sin,
pray for us
Queen of the most
holy Rosary,
pray for us
Queen of peace,
pray for us
Lamb of God, who takes
away the sins of the world
spare us, O Lord
Lamb of God, who takes
away the sins of the world
graciously hear us, O Lord
Lamb of God, who takes
away the sins of the world
have mercy on us
Pray for us, most holy
Mother of God,
*that we may be made
worthy of the promises
of Christ*

Let us pray

Lord God, give to your people the joy of continual health in mind and body. With the prayers of the Virgin Mary to help us, guide us through the sorrows of this life to eternal happiness in the life to come. Grant this through our Lord Jesus Christ, your Son, who lives and reigns with you and the Holy Spirit, one God, for ever and ever. Amen.

St Louis de Montfort's Prayer to Mary

Hail Mary, beloved daughter of the Eternal Father. Hail Mary, admirable Mother of the Son. Hail Mary, faithful spouse of the Holy Spirit. Hail Mary, my Mother, my loving mistress, my powerful sovereign. Hail, my joy, my glory, my heart and my soul. You are all mine by mercy, and I am yours by justice. But I am not yet sufficiently yours. I now give myself wholly to you without keeping anything back for others or myself. If you see anything in me that does not belong to you, I beseech you to take it and make yourself the absolute Mistress of all that is mine.

Destroy in me all that may displease God; root it up and bring it to nothing. Place and cultivate in me everything that is pleasing to you. May the light of your faith dispel the darkness of my mind. May your profound humility take the place of my pride; may your sublime contemplation check the distractions of my wandering imagination. May the continuous sight of God fill my memory with his presence; may the burning love of your heart inflame the lukewarmness of mine. May your virtues take the place of my sins; may your merits be my only adornment in the sight of God and make up for all that is wanting in me. Finally, dearly beloved Mother, grant, if it be possible, that I may have no other spirit but yours to know Jesus, and his divine will; that I may have no other soul but yours to praise and glorify God; that I may have no other heart but yours to love God with a love as pure and ardent as yours.

I do not ask you for visions, revelations, sensible devotions, or spiritual pleasures. It is your privilege to see God clearly, it is your privilege to enjoy heavenly bliss; it is your privilege to triumph gloriously in heaven at the right hand of your Son and to hold absolute sway over angels, men, and demons. It is your privilege to dispose of all the gifts of God, just as you will. Such, O heavenly Mary, is the "best part", which the Lord has given you, and which shall never be taken away from you - and this thought fills my heart with joy. As for my part here below, I wish for no other than that which was yours, to believe sincerely without spiritual pleasures, to suffer joyfully without human consolation, to die continually to myself without respite, and to work zealously and unselfishly for you until death, as the humblest of your servants. The only grace I beg of you, for myself, is that every moment of the day, and every moment of my life, I may say, "Amen, so be it, to all that you are doing in heaven. Amen, so be it, to all you did while on earth. Amen, so be it, to all you are doing in my soul," so that you alone may fully glorify Jesus in me for time and eternity. Amen.

Litany of the Sacred Heart

Lord, have mercy
Lord, have mercy
Christ, have mercy
Christ, have mercy
Lord, have mercy
Lord, have mercy
Christ, hear us
Christ, hear us
Christ, graciously hear us
Christ, graciously hear us
God the Father of Heaven,
have mercy on us
God the Son, redeemer of the world,
have mercy on us
God, the Holy Spirit,
have mercy on us
Holy Trinity, One God,
have mercy on us
Heart of Jesus,
Son of the Eternal Father,
have mercy on us
Heart of Jesus,
formed by the Holy Spirit
in the womb of the
Virgin Mother,
have mercy on us

Heart of Jesus,
substantially united to the
Word of God,
have mercy on us
Heart of Jesus, of infinite
majesty,
have mercy on us
Heart of Jesus, sacred
temple of God,
have mercy on us
Heart of Jesus, tabernacle
of the Most High,
have mercy on us
Heart of Jesus, house of
God and gate of heaven,
have mercy on us
Heart of Jesus, burning
furnace of charity,
have mercy on us
Heart of Jesus, abode of
justice and love,
have mercy on us
Heart of Jesus, full of
goodness and love,
have mercy on us

Heart of Jesus,
abyss of all virtues,
have mercy on us
Heart of Jesus, most
worthy of all praise,
have mercy on us
Heart of Jesus, king and
centre of all hearts,
have mercy on us
Heart of Jesus, in whom
are all treasures of
wisdom and knowledge,
have mercy on us
Heart of Jesus,
in whom dwells the
fullness of divinity,
have mercy on us
Heart of Jesus,
in whom the Father
was well pleased,
have mercy on us
Heart of Jesus,
of whose fullness we
have all received,
have mercy on us

Heart of Jesus, desire of
the everlasting hills,
have mercy on us
Heart of Jesus, patient and
most merciful,
have mercy on us
Heart of Jesus, enriching
all who invoke you,
have mercy on us
Heart of Jesus,
fountain of life and
holiness,
have mercy on us
Heart of Jesus,
propitiation for our sins,
have mercy on us
Heart of Jesus, loaded
down with opprobrium,
have mercy on us
Heart of Jesus,
bruised for our offences,
have mercy on us
Heart of Jesus,
obedient to death,
have mercy on us

Heart of Jesus,
pierced with a lance,
have mercy on us
Heart of Jesus,
source of all consolation,
have mercy on us
Heart of Jesus,
our life and resurrection,
have mercy on us
Heart of Jesus, our peace
and our reconciliation,
have mercy on us
Heart of Jesus,
victim for our sins,
have mercy on us
Heart of Jesus, salvation
of those who trust in you,
have mercy on us
Heart of Jesus, hope of
those who die in you,
have mercy on us
Heart of Jesus,
delight of all the Saints,
have mercy on us

Lamb of God,
who takes away the sins
of the world,
have mercy on us
Lamb of God,
who takes away the sins
of the world,
have mercy on us

Lamb of God,
who takes away the sins
of the world,
have mercy on us
Jesus, meek and humble
of heart
*make our hearts like
unto yours*

Let us pray

Almighty and eternal God, look upon the heart of your most beloved Son and upon the praises and satisfaction that he offers you in the name of sinners; and to those who implore your mercy. In your great goodness, grant forgiveness in the name of the same Jesus Christ, your Son, who lives and reigns with you and the Holy Spirit, now and forever. Amen.

St Louis de Montfort's Prayer to Jesus

O most loving Jesus, allow me to pour out my gratitude before you, for the grace you have bestowed upon me in giving me to your holy Mother through the devotion of holy slavery, that she may be my advocate in the presence of your majesty and my support in my extreme misery. Alas, O Lord! I am so wretched that without this dear Mother I should be certainly lost. Yes, Mary is necessary for me at your side and everywhere: that she may appease your just wrath, because I have so often offended you; that she may save me from the eternal punishment of your justice, which I deserve; that she may contemplate you, speak to you, pray to you, approach you and please you; that she may help me to save my soul and the souls of others; in short, Mary is necessary for me that I may always do your holy will and seek your greater glory in all things. Ah, would that I could proclaim throughout the whole world the mercy that you have shown to me! Would that everyone might know I should be already damned, were it not for Mary! Would that I might offer worthy thanksgiving for so great a blessing! Mary is in me. Oh, what a treasure! Oh, what a consolation! And shall I not be entirely hers? Oh, what ingratitude! My dear Saviour, send me death rather than such a calamity, for I would rather die than live without belonging entirely to Mary. With St John the Evangelist at the foot of the Cross, I have taken her a thousand times for my own and as many times have given myself to her; but if I have not yet done it as you, dear Jesus, would wish, I now renew this offering as you desire me to renew it. And if you see in my soul or my body anything that does not belong to this august princess, I pray you to take it and cast it far from me, for whatever in me does not belong to Mary is unworthy of you.

O Holy Spirit, grant me all these graces. Plant in my soul the tree of true life, which is Mary; cultivate it and tend it so that it may grow and blossom and bring forth the fruit of life in abundance. O Holy Spirit, give me great devotion to Mary, your faithful spouse; give me great confidence in her maternal heart and an abiding refuge in her mercy, so that, by her, you may truly form in me Jesus Christ, great and mighty, unto the fullness of his perfect age. Amen.

Day of Consecration

Instructions for Consecration

On the day of consecration, either fast, give alms, or offer a votive candle for the good of another (or all of the above); do some spiritual penance and approach the consecration in the spirit of mortification.

Now go to Confession (or, if that is not possible, try to go within a week) and then receive Communion with the intention of giving yourself to Jesus, as a slave of love, by the hands of Mary.

Now pray the words of the consecration on the next two pages. Copy them and have them with you at church, read them after the Mass, and sign your copy of the Act of Consecration.

Every year at least, on the same date, we should renew the consecration following the same exercises. We might also renew it every month or even every day by saying this short prayer: "I am all yours and all I have is yours, O dear Jesus, through Mary, your holy Mother."

Consecration to Jesus through Mary

O Eternal and incarnate Wisdom! O sweetest and most adorable Jesus! True God and true man, only Son of the Eternal Father, and of Mary, always virgin! I adore you profoundly in the bosom and splendours of your Father during eternity; and I adore you also in the virginal bosom of Mary, your most worthy Mother, in the time of your incarnation.

I give you thanks for you have annihilated yourself, taking the form of a slave in order to rescue me from the cruel slavery of the devil. I praise and glorify you for you have been pleased to submit yourself to Mary, your holy Mother, in all things, in order to make me your faithful slave through her. But, alas, ungrateful and faithless as I have been, I have not kept the promises which I made so solemnly to you in my Baptism; I have not fulfilled my obligations; I do not deserve to be called your child, or even your slave; and as there is nothing in me which does not merit your anger and your repulse, I dare not come by myself before your most holy and august majesty. It is on this account that I have recourse to the intercession of your most holy Mother, whom you have given me for a mediatrix with you. It is through her that I hope to obtain from you contrition, the pardon of my sins, and the acquisition and preservation of wisdom.

Hail, then, O Immaculate Mary, living tabernacle of the Divinity, where the Eternal Wisdom willed to be hidden and to be adored by angels and by men! Hail, O Queen of Heaven and earth, to whose empire everything is subject which is under God. Hail, O sure refuge of sinners, whose mercy fails no one. Hear the desires which I have of the Divine Wisdom; and for that end receive the vows and offerings which in my lowliness I present to you.

I, *(write your name here)*, a faithless sinner, renew and ratify today in your hands the vows of my Baptism; I renounce forever Satan, his works and empty promises; and I give myself entirely to Jesus Christ, the Incarnate Wisdom, to carry my cross after him all the days of my life, and to be more faithful to him than I have ever been before. In the presence of all the heavenly court I choose you this day for my Mother and Mistress. I deliver and consecrate to you, as your slave, my body and soul, my goods, both interior and exterior, and even the value of all my good actions, past, present and future; leaving to you the entire and full right of disposing of me, and all that belongs to me, without exception, according to your good pleasure, for the greater glory of God in time and in eternity.

Receive, O compassionate Virgin, this little offering of my slavery, in honour of, and in union with, that subjection which the Eternal Wisdom deigned to have to your maternity; in homage to the power which both of you have over this poor sinner, and in thanksgiving for the privileges with which the Holy Trinity has favoured you. I declare that I wish henceforth, as your true slave, to seek your honour and to obey you in all things.

O admirable Mother, present me to your dear Son as his eternal slave, so that as he has redeemed me by you, by you he may receive me! O Mother of mercy, grant me the grace to obtain the true Wisdom of God; and for that end receive me among those who you love and teach, who you lead, nourish and protect as your children and your slaves.

O faithful Virgin, make me in all things so perfect a disciple, imitator and slave of the Incarnate Wisdom, Jesus Christ your Son, that I may attain, by your intercession and by your example, to the fullness of his age on earth and of his glory in heaven. Amen.

Signed: Date:

(Sign and date your name here)

Endnotes

St Louis de Montfort's writings have been very often reprinted, and are available in numerous editions. For this reason, references for passages quoted in the text are to the standard chapters into which his various works are divided, rather than to page numbers of particular editions.

[1] *Secret of Mary*, c.3
[2] *Secret of Mary*, c.4
[3] *Love of Eternal Wisdom*, c.194
[4] *Love of Eternal Wisdom*, c.107
[5] *Love of Eternal Wisdom*, c.10.2
[6] *Letter to the Friends of the Cross*, c.7
[7] *Secret of the Rosary*, c.23
[8] *True Devotion to the Blessed Virgin, Mary*, c.135
[9] *True Devotion*, c.89
[10] *True Devotion*, c.178
[11] *True Devotion*, c.50
[12] *Love of Eternal Wisdom*, c.98
[13] *True Devotion*, c.127
[14] *True Devotion*, c.255
[15] *True Devotion*, cc.99-100
[16] *True Devotion*, c.78
[17] *True Devotion*, c.78
[18] *Secret of Mary*, c.36
[19] *True Devotion*, c.81
[20] *True Devotion*, c.5
[21] *True Devotion*, c.44
[22] *True Devotion*, c.52
[23] *Secret of Mary*, cc.11-12
[24] *True Devotion*, c.157
[25] *True Devotion*, c.78
[26] *Secret of Mary*, c.57
[27] *True Devotion*, c.219
[28] *True Devotion*, c.61
[29] *Secret of the Rosary*, c.72
[30] *True Devotion*, c.139
[31] *Love of Eternal Wisdom*, c.169
[32] *Friends of the Cross*, c.57
[33] *Love of Eternal Wisdom*, c.71
[34] *True Devotion*, c.56-59

Calendar of possible consecration dates

Start Date	Marian Feast Day on which to finish	End Date
29th November	Mary Mother of God	1st January
6th December	Our Lady of Prompt Succour	8th January
19th December	Our Lady of Consolation	21st January
21st December	Espousal of the Virgin Mary	23rd January
22nd December	Our Lady of Tears	24th January
31st December	Presentation of the Lord	2nd February
9th January	Our Lady of Lourdes	11th February
20th February	Annunciation	25th March
24th March	Our Lady of Good Counsel	26th April
26th March	Feast of St Louis de Montfort	28th April
10th April	Our Lady of Fatima	13th May
21st April	Our Lady Help of Christians	24th May
28th April	Visitation	31st May
7th May	Our Lady of Grace	9th June
25th May	Our Lady of Perpetual Help	27th June
30th May	Visitation by Mary to Elizabeth	2nd July
13th June	Our Lady of Mount Carmel	16th July
15th June	Humility of the Blessed Virgin Mary	17th July
30th June	Our Lady of the Angels	2nd August
4th July	Our Lady of the Snows	5th August
11th July	Our Lady, Refuge of Sinners	13th August
13th July	Assumption	15th August
19th July	Our Lady of Knock	21st August

Start Date	Marian Feast Day on which to finish	End Date
20th July	Queenship of Mary	22nd August
6th August	Birth of Mary	8th September
10th August	Most Holy Name of Mary	12th September
13th August	Our Lady of Sorrows	15th September
22nd August	Our Lady of Mercy	24th September
29th August	Holy Protection of the Mother of God	1st October
2nd September	Our Lady of the Rosary	7th October
5th September	Our Lady of Good Remedy	8th October
8th September	Maternity of the Blessed Virgin Mary	11th October
13th September	Purity of the Blessed Virgin Mary	16th October
19th October	Presentation of the Blessed Virgin Mary	21st November
5th November	Immaculate Conception	8th December
9th November	Our Lady of Guadalupe	12th December
16th November	Expectation of the Blessed Virgin Mary	18th December